No Lex 12-12

# Curiosity

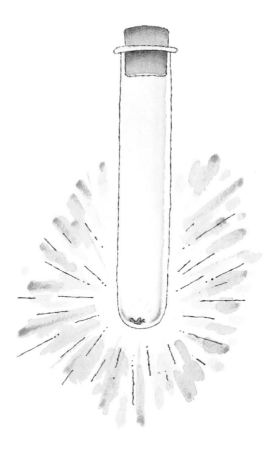

# Curiosity
## The Story of Marie Curie

*by*

Peter Murray

*Illustrated by*

Leon Baxter

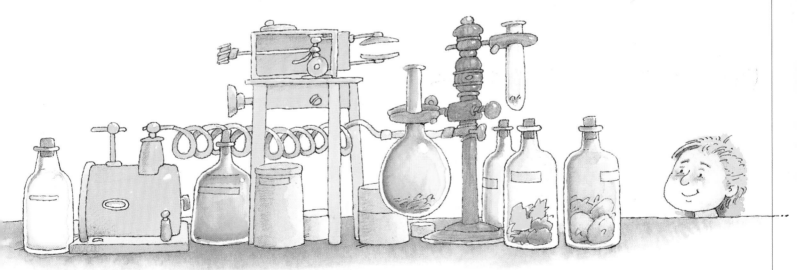

The Child's World®

**Library of Congress Cataloging-in-Publication Data**
Murray, Peter. 1952 Sept. 29
Curiosity: the story of Marie Curie / Peter Murray.
p. cm.
Summary: Explores the life of the Polish-born chemist, with an emphasis on
the role played by curiosity in her discovery of radium.

ISBN 1-56766-229-3

1. Curie, Marie, 1867-1934--Juvenile literature.
2. Chemists--Poland-- Biography--Juvenile literature.
[1. Curie, Marie. 1867-1934. 2. Chemists. 3. Women--Biography.] I. Title.
QD 22.C8M85 1996
540'.92
[B]--DC20
95-42268
CIP
AC

# Contents

# "What Are These Things?"

In the year 1871, in a small
apartment in Warsaw, Poland, a
little girl sat before a tall cabinet,
staring through its glass doors. Her
name was Marya Sklodowska. She had bright
yellow hair and a plump face. She was four years old.

Inside the cabinet, she saw many wonderful things. There were
glass tubes and bottles, and a balance with brass weights. There
were beautiful crystals, and prettily colored rocks, and a strange,
complicated machine. She touched the glass doors with her small
fingers. She wanted to play with the things in the cabinet, but the
doors were locked.

A few feet away, her father sat at his desk reading a book.

"Father," she asked, "What are these things I see in the cabinet?"

Her father put down his book. "That is my *physics apparatus*," he told her.

"Physics apparatus?" She repeated the words slowly, for she had never heard them before. They had a magical sound, though she did not know what they meant.

"What is physics?" she asked. Her father sighed. "My goodness, Marya!" he said. "You are a very curious little girl!"

## What Is *Curiosity*?

*Curiosity* is the desire to know, the desire to learn. When you wonder about something—what is on the other side of a door, or who your teacher will be next year, or where frogs go in the winter—that's curiosity. Curiosity is what makes us want to find out about the world around us.

Marya's father was a schoolteacher. He told her that *physics* was the science of matter and energy. He used the *apparatus* in the cabinet for teaching his students the natural laws of the universe. The scale was for weighing minerals and other substances. The strange-looking machine was an electroscope, used to measure electricity.

Marya did not understand all her father told her, but she listened to every word. One day, she thought, I will have my own *physics apparatus.*

Marya was still too young to go to school, but she was very smart. One day her older sister, Bronya, was trying to learn to read. Marya watched her big sister struggling to sound out the words in her schoolbook. Marya took the book from her sister and began to read out loud. Her parents could not believe it!

Marya had taught herself to read!

# Learning, the Hard Way

In the late 1800s, Poland was ruled by Russia. Polish children spent most of their school days learning to speak Russian and learning Russian history. It was against the law to teach the children about Poland. They were not allowed to speak Polish in the classroom. They were not taught sciences such as physics and mathematics. Marya's father, who taught at the high school, argued with the Russian headmaster and was fired.

The family had little money, but that was the least of their problems. In 1875 Marya's sisters Bronya and Sophia both caught a deadly disease called *typhus.* Bronya recovered, but Sophia died in January, 1876, at the age of 13. Two years later, Marya's mother died from tuberculosis.

Saddened by the loss of her sister and mother, Marya tried to learn as much as she could at school. It gave her great pleasure to learn something new every day. Turning the pages of a book was an adventure. What lovely new facts would the next page reveal? What new lands would she visit? Marya had tremendous powers of concentration. When she was reading, nothing else mattered. Even when the other children were running around, playing and shouting, Marya was able to study.

When she was 16 years old, Marya won a gold medal for being the best student at her school. This was very unusual, for at that time girls were not encouraged to study hard. Most girls did not finish high school, and almost none went on to college. But the Sklodowska girls were different. Both Bronya and Marya planned to go to the university of the Sorbonne, in Paris, France. Bronya wanted to study medicine, and Marya wanted to become a scientist. But how could they afford to live in Paris? The family had no money. Somehow, they must find a way.

Bronya and Marya came up with a plan. Because Bronya was older, she would go to Paris first. Marya would stay in Poland and work as a governess, living with a wealthy Polish family and teaching their children. Then, when Bronya became a doctor, she would pay to bring Marya to Paris! It would take five years for Bronya to finish school, but what else could they do? So, in 1886, Bronya climbed aboard the train to Paris, and Marya went to work as a governess.

# Paris!

**M**arya's years as a governess were difficult for her. At night, she tried to teach herself by reading books about chemistry, physics, and mathematics. But the books were old and out of date. She needed a laboratory for her science experiments. She could not wait to quit her job and go to Paris!

In 1890, a letter arrived from Bronya. She had fallen in love with a French doctor, and they planned to marry. Soon she could afford to bring Marya to Paris and offer her a place to live.

One year later, Marya was in Paris and enrolled in the university of the Sorbonne. This was what she had always wanted! She could use all of the libraries. She could go into the lecture halls, where great ideas were freely discussed. Soon after arriving in Paris, she became known as Marie, the French form of Marya.

> **"A**ll my mind was centered on my studies. All that I saw and learned that was new delighted me. It was like a whole new world opened to me, the world of science, which I was at last permitted to know in liberty."
>
> —*Marie Sklodowska, 1892*

Marie's education at the Sorbonne was not easy. She knew how to speak French, but the professors talked very fast. She had trouble understanding them. Her education in Poland had not taught her enough. She was 23 years old, but she knew less than many of the young French students.

But Marie was determined to succeed. She wanted more than anything else to become a scientist. She wanted to explore the unknown secrets of the natural world. She spent long hours at the Sorbonne, working hard to catch up.

And she did.

In July of 1893, at the age of 25, Marie took her physics exam. She got the best score of all the students! One year later, she received her degree in mathematics, finishing second in her class.

# "His Smile ... Inspired Confidence"

One day Marie met a man named Pierre Curie. Pierre taught physics at the Paris School of Physics and Chemistry. Marie did not want to like him. She had no time for men. Her studies were far more important. But she could not take her eyes off Pierre. Later, she said, "I was struck by the expression of his clear gaze . . . his smile, at once grave and young, inspired confidence."

Pierre was equally struck by Marie. He was impressed by her enthusiasm and her quick mind. He shared her love of science, and her desire to learn more.

The two quickly became friends. Pierre talked of marriage, but Marie was not interested. She planned to return to Poland after school. She felt it was her duty to bring her new knowledge back to her people.

Pierre would not give up so easily. He was determined to marry Marie!

In 1895, Marie decided to marry Pierre and stay in France. Marie Sklodowska became Marie Curie. Pierre and Marie took a bicycle honeymoon, pedaling their way across the beautiful French countryside.

"It would be a fine thing, to pass our lives near to each other; hypnotized by our dreams; *your* patriotic dream, *our* humanitarian dream, and *our* scientific dream."
—*Pierre Curie, in a letter to Marie, August, 1894.*

# A Mysterious New Subject

**D**uring the following years, while Pierre studied the properties of crystals and taught at his school, Marie studied the magnetic properties of steel. She also had a baby girl named Irene. Marie loved her new daughter, but she did not let motherhood stop her from studying science. She planned to do something no woman had ever done before: She wanted to become a Doctor of Science.

Marie chose a new subject for her doctoral degree. Her decision would forever change her life—in both good ways and bad.

**T**here is an old saying: "*Curiosity* killed the cat." Cats have a way of looking into dark corners. Sometimes they don't like what they find. Curious people sometimes have the same problem.

A scientist named Henri Becquerel had discovered that uranium, a heavy, silvery white element, sent off rays that could darken photographic film. These invisible rays could pass right through wood, glass, or iron—but not lead! What were these mysterious rays? Marie decided to find out.

Marie measured the strength of the rays using a machine built by Pierre. She decided to call the rays "radiation."

She asked herself, "Are there other elements that give off similar rays?"

An *element* is a pure substance that cannot be broken down into different substances. Uranium, gold, carbon, and oxygen are examples of elements. The air you breathe is made up of many different elements. So is a rock you pick up off the ground. Elements are the building blocks of our universe. When Marie began her search, fewer than 90 elements were known. Today, there are 109.

Marie discovered that *pitchblende*, the ore that produces uranium, gave off more radiation than it should. When all its uranium was removed, pitchblende still gave off rays! In 1898, she realized that pitchblende must contain a small amount of an unknown radioactive element. She had to know what it was!

Both Pierre and Marie were excited by this new possibility. They decided to work together, to search for this mysterious new substance.

For the next year, they worked with pitchblende, heating it, straining it, rinsing it with acids, crystallizing it, and breaking it down into its component elements. Each time they separated out an element they did not want, they got closer to their goal. In 1898, they discovered that there were not one, but *two* new elements in the pitchblende. One, they named polonium, after Marie's native Poland. The other, which gave out the strongest rays of all, they called *radium*.

The discovery of these new elements, especially the powerful radium, was tremendously exciting. But to study this new substance, they needed to make it as pure as possible. They knew that the radium was present in the pitchblende, but they had not yet purified it. The problem was that the amount of radium in pitchblende was so small! To find enough of it to study, they would need a *lot* of pitchblende.

The Curies did not have much money. But their excitement and curiosity about this new element never wavered. What would radium look like? Marie hoped that it would turn out to be a beautiful color, like gold.

The head of Pierre's college let them take over an old shed on the school grounds. It was cold and drafty, and the roof leaked. Their laboratory equipment was crude. Their only light came from a dirty skylight. But to Pierre and Marie, it was the key to realizing their dream. Sacks and sacks of pitchblende were delivered to the shed. For four long years, the Curies worked, melting down tons of pitchblende, reducing it with acids and other chemicals, searching for a few grains of pure radium. The work was long, hard, dirty, and uncomfortable, but the Curies were driven by their need to know.

> " It was in that miserable old shed that the best and happiest days of our life were spent, entirely consecrated to work."
>
> —*Marie Curie*

# A Deadly Secret

As the Curies' radium samples became more and more refined, their excitement grew. In 1902, after refining several tons of pitchblende, they finally succeeded in producing one-tenth of a gram of pure radium in a test tube—an amount smaller than an apple seed. The pure radium was 1 million times more radioactive than uranium! One dark night Marie and Pierre stood in their shed and noticed a soft blue light surrounding the test tube. The radium was glowing! They could see the radiation!

"You see," said Pierre. "It is as you wished. The radium is truly beautiful!"

What neither Pierre nor Marie realized was that the beautiful blue glow was slowly killing them.

They had reached their goal, but there was more work to be done. If only they didn't feel so sick! Both Pierre and Marie had sores on their fingers. They were tired all the time. Pierre's joints ached constantly. Marie had lost weight. They both developed a cough that would not go away.

We know now that the Curies were suffering from radiation sickness, but at that time, they had no idea what was wrong with them. Marie and Pierre continued to research the properties of radium. Pierre discovered that items placed near the radium became radioactive themselves. In fact, the notebooks the Curies used became so radioactive that they eventually had to be locked away in a lead cabinet. Pierre also learned that contact with radium could destroy human cells. Here was the reason for the sores on their fingers!

Pierre wondered whether radium could be used to destroy cancer cells. Tests by French doctors were encouraging, and radium was put to use saving lives—even as it was killing Marie and Pierre!

Today, doctors still use radiation to treat patients. *Radiotherapy* is used to destroy cancerous cells. *Scintigraphy* uses radioactive particles to help doctors look inside a patient's body. The work of the Curies has saved many thousands of lives.

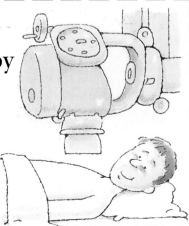

# Triumph . . . and Tragedy

**M**arie's work with radium won her a Doctor of Science degree in 1903. She was the first woman to achieve such an honor. Later that same year, she and Pierre won the Nobel Prize for physics— one of the most important awards in science. Pierre was given a special professorship at the Sorbonne. Marie had shown the world that you did not have to be a man to make great scientific discoveries. At last they had money and a comfortable place to work!

Marie gave birth to a second daughter in 1904. This was a proud and happy time for the Curies, even though they continued to suffer from the effects of radiation. Marie divided her time between her laboratory work and teaching.

In 1906, Pierre tried to cross a street in Paris and was run down by a speeding horse-drawn wagon. Marie felt as if her life had ended, too. She was 39 years old, with two young daughters, and her husband was suddenly gone from her life.

When Marie's *curiosity* drove her to study uranium's mysterious rays, she was looking into a whole new world of science. She did not know that her choice would eventually harm both her and her husband. But even if she had known the dangers of radiation, Marie Curie probably would have studied it anyway. "After all," she might say, "How else are we to learn?"

# The Atomic Age

**P**ierre was gone, but Marie's life was just beginning. She was given Pierre's professorship at the Sorbonne. She became the first woman to hold such a post in the sciences. She taught the world's first course on radioactivity. In 1911, she was awarded another Nobel Prize—this time in chemistry—making her the only person to win the prize twice!

In 1914, war broke out all across Europe. With most of the French people involved in the war effort, Marie's scientific research came to a halt. Marie figured out that portable X-ray units could be mounted on trucks and driven to the front lines. The X-ray machines could be used to save soldiers' lives. At the end of the war, Marie and her daughter Irene were given the Medal of Courage for their work.

Marie Curie's curiosity led us into the Atomic Age. Without her research we would not be able to cure cancer with radiotherapy. We would not have nuclear power plants, which provide much of the world's electricity. And we would not have the atomic bomb.

For the last 20 years of her life, Marie continued to make scientific discoveries. During this time she continued to suffer from the effects of radiation. Her eyesight began to fail, and she became weaker with each passing year. Her curiosity, her desire to learn, and her passion for science kept her going. Considering the amount of radiation she must have absorbed, it is remarkable that she lived so long. In 1934, she died from leukemia caused by exposure to radium. She was 67 years old.

> "The question can be raised whether mankind benefits from knowing the secrets of Nature. Will it profit from it? Or will this knowledge be harmful? I am one of those who believe that mankind will derive more good than harm from new discoveries."
>
> —*Pierre Curie*

# Study Guide

*Marie Curie's life was filled with successes, failures, happiness, and sadness. When we read about great men and women, we see how the choices they made affected their lives.*

1. Which of these qualities do you think are most important?

 Intelligence

Strength

Self-confidence

Fairness

Imagination

Courage

 Generosity

Perseverance

Love

Curiosity

 Patience

Kindness

Which qualities do you think were most important to Marie Curie?

2. After her death, Marie Curie's research into radioactivity led to the development of the atomic bomb. In 1945, atomic bombs were dropped on the cities of Hiroshima and Nagasaki in Japan. The bombing brought World War II to an end, but 150,000 people were killed. Do you think that Marie would have wanted the atomic bomb?

3. During most of Marie Curie's lifetime, women in France and England did not have the right to vote. How do you think Marie felt about that?

4. Marie was a very practical woman. She did not like fancy clothes or jewelry, and she kept her hair tied back so that it would not get in her way. She preferred dark-colored dresses because they would not show burns or acid stains. For her wedding, she bought a plain, dark blue dress so that she could wear it later for her laboratory work. If Marie were alive today, what do you think she would be wearing?

5. When Marie Curie lost most of her eyesight from exposure to radium, she refused to believe that radium was the cause. Why do you think such a smart woman would make such a mistake?

# Study Guide Answers

1. Marie Curie might have had a hard time answering this question. How could her strength and courage be more important than her love for Pierre? What good would her intelligence be if she did not have self-confidence and perseverance? We are all a mixture of qualities, both good and bad.

2. Marie spent the last decades of her life using radiation to cure diseases and relieve the suffering of wounded soldiers. No one can say for sure what her thoughts about the bomb would have been. She probably would have found it difficult to see the results of her research used to kill so many people. At the same time, she would have been glad to see the war ended. What do *you* think?

3. Marie believed that women were equal to men, and that they should have the same rights. In her first lecture at the Sorbonne she said, "Today has seen the celebration of a victory for feminism. If a woman is allowed to teach advanced studies to both sexes, where afterward will be the pretended superiority of man? I tell you, the time is near when women will become human beings."

4. Many woman today share Marie Curie's practicality and love of science, and they wear all different kinds of clothing. If Marie were alive today, who knows what she would be wearing? Maybe she would wear blue jeans and a sweatshirt. Maybe she would wear that same navy blue wedding dress!

5. Sometimes parents refuse to believe that their children can do bad things. Maybe radium was like one of Marie's children. She had brought it into the world, she loved its beautiful light, and she could see only its good qualities.

## Marie Curie Time Line

**November 7, 1867**  Marya Sklodowska (sklaw-DAWF-skah) is born in Warsaw, Poland

**1891**  Marya goes to Paris to study at the Sorbonne University. She becomes known as Marie instead of Marya.

**1895**  Marie marries Pierre Curie.

**1898**  Marie and Pierre discover polonium and radium.

**1903** Marie and Pierre win the Nobel Prize for Physics for the discovery of radioactivity. Marie is the first woman to win the Prize for physics.

**1906**  Pierre Curie dies in an accident.

**1906**  Marie becomes the first female professor to teach at the Sorbonne University.

**1911**  Marie wins the Nobel Prize for Chemistry for her discovery of radium and polonium. She is the first person to receive two Nobel Prizes.

**July 4, 1934**  Marie Curie dies in France.